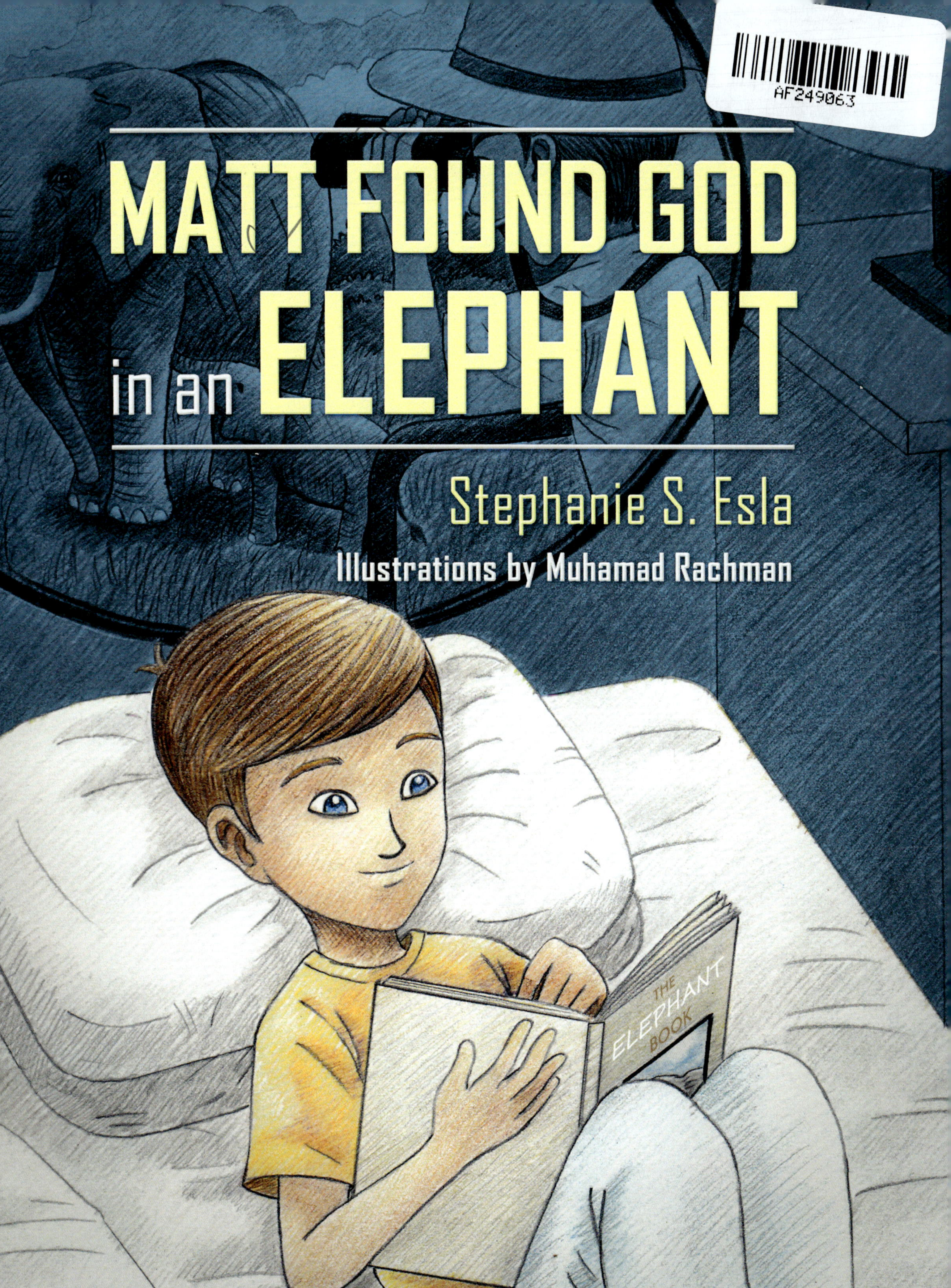

MATT FOUND GOD
in an ELEPHANT
Stephanie S. Esla
Illustrations by Muhamad Rachman
THE ELEPHANT BOOK
AF249063

The opinions expressed in this manuscript are solely the opinions of the author and do not represent the opinions or thoughts of the publisher. The author has represented and warranted full ownership and/or legal right to publish all the materials in this book.

Matt Found God in an Elephant
All Rights Reserved.
Copyright © 2014 Stephanie S. Esla
v5.0

Illustrated by: Muhamad Rachman
Illustrations © 2014 Outskirts Press, Inc. All rights reserved - used with permission.

This book may not be reproduced, transmitted, or stored in whole or in part by any means, including graphic, electronic, or mechanical without the express written consent of the publisher except in the case of brief quotations embodied in critical articles and reviews.

S.S.E. Publishing

Paperback ISBN: 978-0-578-13354-6
Hardback ISBN: 978-0-578-13355-3

Library of Congress Control Number: 2013955631

PRINTED IN THE UNITED STATES OF AMERICA

Dedicated to Alan, Sean & Ali

THIS BOOK BELONGS TO

M att was just a little boy when he found himself drawn to elephants. The magic and mystery of these majestic creatures fascinated Matt. Matt heard tales of men going to Asia and Africa to view these creatures in their natural habitat, and he dreamt that one day it would be him going on that journey.

att's only chance to view the elephants was at the circus or at the local zoo. At the big top, the cotton candy, trapeze artists, flashy lights, and the mighty elephant doing a handstand did not seem to add up correctly, Matt thought. Every time he questioned his parents, his question was answered with the same monotone answer: "Honey, this is their home. They are happy here." But, there was something not quite right about this mighty giant wearing a tutu and doing handstands.

FRICA
THE AFRICA BOOK
THE HOLY BIBLE
THE ELEPHANT BOOK
ENCYCLOPEDIA
ENCYCLOPEDIA
ENCYCLOPEDIA
ENCYCLOPEDIA

And so with little Matt's curiosity and compassion for elephants, his parents decided it was time to take a trip to the continent of Africa. Matt was overjoyed, as he was finally going to see the elephants in herds as he had read about in the storybooks.

THE AFRICA BOOK
THE HOLY BIBLE
THE ELEPHANT BOOK
ENCYCLOPE
ENCYCLOPE
ENCYCLOPE
ENCYCLOPE

n anticipation, Matt spent many nights reading about these majestic giants and their bond and unity to the other members of their herd. He learned about the natural and indestructible bond of a mother elephant and her calf. Matt also learned that, like human children, elephant calves have babysitters, too. Most of the time, it would be the grandmother or the aunt of the calf. *"Wow!"* he thought. This brought little Matt's enthusiasm for the trip to another level of excitement!

U.S AIRWAYS

Finally, the day came. And the plane was on its final descent to touch down on the African plains. The excitement was unbearable for Matt! Upon arriving in Botswana, a huge herd of giraffes immediately welcomed Matt as a taxi drove them away from the airport. He was amazed that giraffes roamed their natural habitat on one side of the highway while high rises peppered the other. He could not believe his eyes. With all this excitement, he was sure that he would finally satisfy his own insatiable curiosity about these mighty creatures.

It would be some time until Matt was able to spot an elephant. His parents had planned several animal encounters, but Matt found himself disappointed since none of the encounters included elephants. There seemed to be plenty of wild animals roaming around the camp site—including a very old hippo—but there was just no sign of the magnificent giant. Nevertheless, Matt did not give up hope, knowing his parents always thought of everything. He was confident that the best part of the African trip was yet to come.

And so at 6:00 a.m. on the fourth day in Botswana, it was finally time for Matt and his family to experience their first safari.

With a cup of hot chocolate and a flashlight in hand, Matt was up and ready to board the safari vehicle. Matt's parents could sense his excitement and anticipation as he quickly covered himself up with a blanket and turned on his camera.

As the safari vehicle moved away from the camp site, Matt's enthusiasm increased quickly with the floral, piney, grassy smell that had brewed so beautifully in the forest.

And so their safari began, and they saw endless families of monkeys, giraffes, deer, lions, and hyenas—and yet, there was no sign of the mighty elephant. Matt, full of wonder, was questioning his mom and dad as to why and to where the elephants might have migrated. "Where are they, Mom? Where are they, Dad?" he repeatedly asked. But they did not have an answer, and the knowledgeable guide just seemed distracted by the other guests.

On the last day of their visit in Botswana, curious little Matt decided to approach the wise old man smoking a rolled-up piece of yesterday's newspaper. He wanted to track down the mysterious region of the grand elephants.

Bently was the man's name and he was a third-generation tour guide in Botswana. So Matt asked wise old Bently the whereabouts of the mighty African elephants. Bently, without a word to say, and a blank face, and smoke coming out of his nostrils like an antique chimney, looked up and pointed to the sky.

As Matt looked up, he realized that old Bently was pointing at a cloud that was shaped like the mighty elephant: a big strong body, long tusks...and most distinct of all, the large ears were beautifully defined in the nimbus cloud.

Despite his brief conversation with wise and old Bently, Matt was still not able to understand what the reason was and why he did not see any elephants in Africa, but it was finally time for Matt and his parents to end their journey.

The next morning, Matt, extremely saddened by his own expectations, boarded the large aircraft to head back home. And as the animals and the trees on the ground were getting smaller and smaller, Matt prayed and asked God what could have happened to the mighty giants and why he was not able to get an answer from anyone.

SAFARI
TOUR
KENYA
(RESCUE THE ELEPHANT)

s the airplane got ready to land just shortly after takeoff, all to Matt's surprise, Matt found himself on another journey.

Little did Matt know that his father had decided to take a detour prior to returning home. He felt the disappointment in Matt's experience, and so in Kenya, he thought he would be able to give little Matt the encounter that he so longed for. Unlike Botswana, there weren't any wild animals next to the airport, but Matt once again found hope of seeing elephants in their natural habitat. Matt's father, realizing his son's determination to see the gentle giant on the continent of Africa, headed straight to a park that offered elephant rides.

Matt got an opportunity to meet Ti, a four-year-old Asian elephant that had been taken from the wilderness in Chiang Mai, Thailand and trained to give rides to the visitors of this park in Meru, Kenya. Matt was saddened once again, questioning his father as to why the elephants were not roaming free, and decided against riding the chained and unhappy elephant. Regardless of the rest of the family's decision to purchase rides and support the elephant conservation efforts, Matt did not wish to support the ride.

Matt decided to go and visit with Ti while the family was getting ready for the free photo that was part of their donation toward the conservation efforts. Matt approached Ti, noticing the cement walls, and wondered if Ti missed being in the wilderness with his family. With some excitement, Matt then noticed that the chained elephant was slowly turning to face him. As their eyes connected, Matt saw fear, loneliness, and a magnificent being, longing to live in green pastures and free of chains. Matt, in tears, could not reason through the overwhelming feeling that came over him, as he did not know where and how to begin helping Ti break out of his shackles and chains.

With tears in his eyes, Matt understood the mystery behind the disappearance of the mighty giant. He finally realized that they had been removed from the wild for the sake of entertainment, and that their home was no longer where it was meant to be. The old man in Botswana and his message in the clouds all came together for Matt, as the old man had given him the message that only God would be able to save this magnificent giant. Matt was overwhelmed by finally finding the answer, which included the hesitation and lack of excitement he felt while watching the humble giant at the zoo and in the circus.

WILDLIFE REHABILITATION
CONSERVATION IN THE WILD
ENCYCLOPEDIA

att realized that this was what God had intended for him to do all along. Convinced of his calling, he began learning more about the wild animals of Africa. Matt had found God in an elephant indeed! His efforts were focused on getting these mighty creatures out of circuses and zoos, and placing them in sanctuaries or introducing them back to the wild.

Not long after Matt graduated college and returned to the beautiful continent of Africa, he met Beth. Matt and Beth would raise orphaned baby elephants and reintroduce them back in the wild. They both believed that God had meant for wild animals to have liberty within nature. Matt and Beth would tell their children and grandchildren about Matt's first journey to the magnificent continent of Africa and how the mighty elephant was saved from extinction. In his stories, Matt also included his close connection to nature, and how he finally found God through the magnificent elephant. Matt enjoyed taking his children and grandchildren on night safaris while sipping hot cocoa under the stars and listening to the elephants' thankful and harmonious sounds of serenity.

"Grandpa, grandpa, can we go see Ti again? We have the blankets and the hot chocolate. And grandpa can you tell us the whole story about how you rescued him?"

The End

CPSIA information can be obtained
at www.ICGtesting.com
Printed in the USA
BVXC01n2300150614
356254BV00001B/8